TIMBER!

WILLIAM JASPERSOHN

Little, Brown and Company   Boston   New York   Toronto   London

Also by
William Jaspersohn:

FOR ERIC SHULZ AND LUCAS SHULZ, WITH LOVE AND THANKS

Acknowledgments

This book could not have been written without the help and cooperation of literally hundreds of people. I particularly wish to thank Jerry Gates, Pat Guillemette, Jonathan Wood, and all the employees at Bell-Gates Lumber, Jeffersonville, Vermont; Mike Paritz at Leo's Small Engine, Morrisville, Vermont; Anita Woodward and all the employees at the Montgomery Schoolhouse Inc., Montgomery, Vermont; Marc Sherman and Victor Collette at Vermont Furniture Works, Stowe, Vermont; John M. Irving and his colleagues at the McNeil Generating Station, Burlington, Vermont; Brian Kinsley and all the employees at the Indian Head Division of Columbia Forest Products, Newport, Vermont; Colleen A. Pope and the fine staff at International Paper, Ticonderoga, New York; and Ron Schwarm of Waterville, Vermont, for the splendid cooperation, counsel, guidance, information, and advice they all gave me during the creation of this book. Meeting every one of them was, for me, one of this project's special pleasures.

I am also indebted to my longtime friend and editor at Little, Brown, John Keller, who coaxed this one out of me with his characteristic patience and élan. My gratitude to him for his efforts on this book's behalf are inestimable.

First Edition

Library of Congress Cataloging-in-Publication Data

Jaspersohn, William.
    Timber! / William Jaspersohn.
      p.   cm.
    Summary: Explains how people and machines turn trees into a variety of wood products.
    ISBN 0-316-45825-2
    1. Wood products—Juvenile literature. 2. Lumbering—Juvenile literature. [1. Wood products. 2. Lumber and lumbering.]
    I. Title.
    TS821.J37 1996
    634.9'8—dc20   95-25194

10 9 8 7 6 5 4 3 2 1

SC

Published simultaneously in Canada by Little, Brown & Company (Canada) Limited

Printed in Hong Kong

IN A FOREST in northern Vermont, trees are being cut for many uses. The forest contains many different kinds of trees. Some are good for lumber, the wood used for building things. Others are good for making paper. Still others are useful as fuel for heat.

SOFTWOODS

WHITE CEDAR

BALSAM

HEMLOCK

RED PINE

WHITE SPRUCE

WHITE PINE

Softwood trees are also called *evergreens* or *conifers.* They stay green all year and do not lose their leaves in the fall. They have needle-like leaves and naked seeds in their cones.

TIMBER FACT

Trees make seeds that fall to the ground or are carried to earth by the wind, animals, and birds. From these seeds sprout new trees, which create new forests. Some people call trees a renewable resource. What do you think they mean by that?

HARDWOODS

ASH

OAK

BEECH

WHITE BIRCH

CHERRY

AMERICAN SUGAR MAPLE

Hardwood trees usually have harder wood than softwood trees do. They shed their leaves in autumn. They grow their seeds in protective casings, such as nut shells (oak, beech), berry pits (cherry), or husks (maple).

THE CHAIN SAW

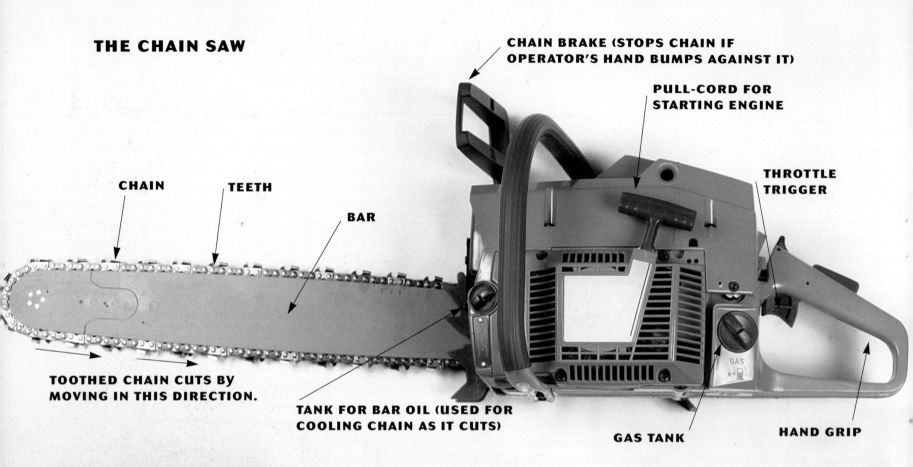

CHAIN BRAKE (STOPS CHAIN IF OPERATOR'S HAND BUMPS AGAINST IT)

PULL-CORD FOR STARTING ENGINE

THROTTLE TRIGGER

CHAIN

TEETH

BAR

TOOTHED CHAIN CUTS BY MOVING IN THIS DIRECTION.

TANK FOR BAR OIL (USED FOR COOLING CHAIN AS IT CUTS)

GAS TANK

HAND GRIP

DID YOU KNOW . . . ?

If you count the growth rings on a stump or log, you can tell a tree's age. This tree is more than forty years old.

People who cut trees for a living are called loggers, or lumberjacks. When loggers cut trees in a forest, they use a variety of machines. The most common cutting machine they use is a chain saw. Its sharp teeth spin fast and cut deep. Chain saws are equipped with several safeguards to help avoid accidents and injuries. But they are still dangerous.

To fell a tree with a chain saw, a logger first makes a wedge cut in it. Then, working carefully, the logger makes a back cut. The tree sways. With a splintering crash, it falls.

Once the tree is on the ground, the logger cuts off its limbs and branches, then loops a length of chain around the log that remains. He attaches the chain to a strong cable. The cable is attached to a powerful machine called a skidder. A skidder can drag many logs at a time. It has big tires and a powerful motor to help it travel over rough ground.

CLEAR-CUTTING

Feller-bunchers are useful for *clear-cutting*, or taking down all the trees on a piece of land. In another type of logging, called *selective cutting*, only some trees are chosen to be cut, while others are left to grow and provide protection for new trees.

To quickly cut many trees in a short time, some loggers use machines called feller-bunchers, or tree shears. These machines have two metal arms for gripping the trees and two powerful blades for cutting them. Feller-bunchers can cut big trees in one bite. Then they lay the cut trees in neat piles.

A grapple skidder collects the trees left along the forest road. With its massive jaws and mighty boom, it moves through the forest like a prehistoric beast. It picks up piles of trees and drags them to an open space in the forest called a log landing.

There, a big saw called a slasher lops the tops off trees that need it. The tops, along with logs that are no good for lumber, are fed into a machine that grinds them into chips. Trailer trucks receive the matchbook-size chips and drive them away to be sold for fuel.

TO CUT OR NOT TO CUT

Some people say trees should be cut because otherwise they would just die of old age and rot away. Other people say trees should be allowed to rot because they put nutrients back into the soil. They also say that forests that have never been cut (called *old-growth forests*) should be left alone. What do you think? Is it enough to scatter the branches of a felled tree, as most loggers do, so that they rot back into the soil? Or should trees not be cut at all?

Logs that aren't chipped are cut to different lengths—from six to twenty feet. When enough good logs have been collected at the landing, a log truck comes and loads them onto its bed with the aid of a long-armed knuckle boom.

17

Meanwhile, trailer trucks deliver the wood chips to places that can burn them for fuel. At an electrical plant that uses them, the chips are moved by bucket loaders into huge piles. When needed, the chips travel up long conveyors to a nine-story boiler. There they are burned to boil water and turn it into steam. The steam spins big blades in the plant's turbine-powered generator. The turbogenerator makes electricity for many cities and towns.

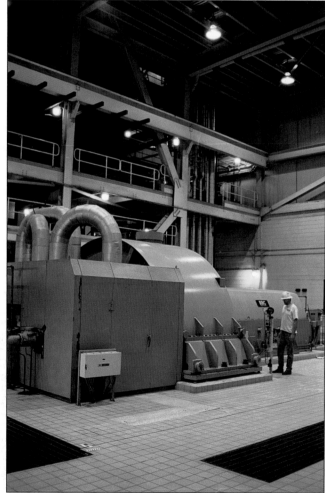

Logs to be used for lumber go to wood mills, where they are scaled (measured for the amount of lumber in them) and graded for quality. Then lifter-buncher machines move them into the mill, where their bark is removed by a machine called a mechanical debarker.

One by one, the peeled logs are sawn into boards. A worker called a sawyer controls the carriage that moves the log through the saw blade. A computer screen in his control booth helps the sawyer decide how wide to make each cut. Afterward, the rough-sawn boards are trimmed on other saws to make them smooth and square.

A worker then slots the boards by grade so that boards of one grade can be stacked and dried together. Once they are dried, the boards are sold for different uses.

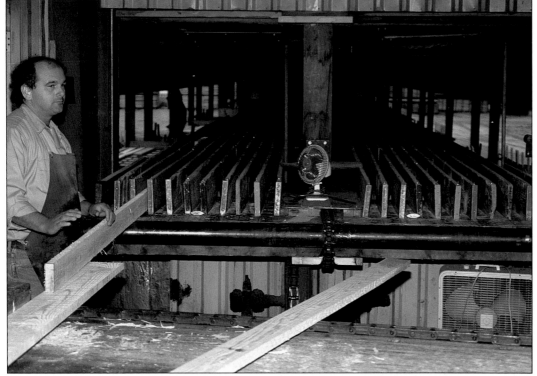

Some mills buy logs from loggers to make thin sheets of wood called veneer. These mills have powerful machines that spin the logs at high speeds. As a log spins, a razor-sharp blade ten feet long cuts the log into one wide, long, floppy ribbon. Later, this ribbon is cut into sheets. Some sheets are glued together to make plywood. Others are glued to different materials to make panels for walls and shelving.

RECYCLING

Not all paper is made directly from trees. More and more, new paper is being made from old, *recycled* paper. Does your community have a paper recycling center? If so, visit it and find out how it works. Offer to be a recycling volunteer. If your community doesn't have a recycling center, write to your community's leaders and work with them to help get one started. Remember: Recycling helps save trees.

At paper mills, truckloads of logs or chips arrive every day. The logs are debarked and chipped, and heaps of chips are cooked in a giant pressure cooker ten stories high. It's called a digester. The digester uses a chemical called cooking liquor to turn the hard chips into a soft, mushy brown pulp. This pulp is then washed, bleached, and mixed with other ingredients until it's a watery white soup.

27

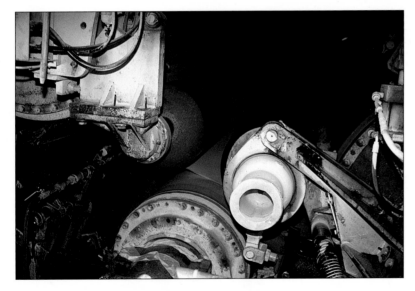

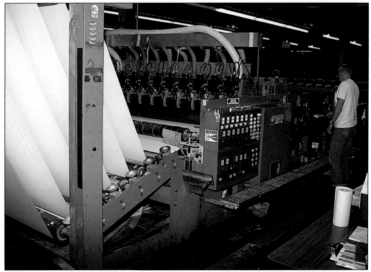

The raw, soupy pulp is sprayed onto a fine-mesh screen moving at forty-five feet per second. As water drains through the screen, the pulp is pressed and dried. The roll of dry paper that comes off the machine is as wide as a highway and as heavy as twelve big cars. It is quickly rewound and cut into smaller rolls. These rolls are either sold directly to customers or are first cut into stacks of paper, then sold. The paper in this book was made by this process. So is most of the other paper made in the world.

TIMBER PRODUCTS

Below is a list of twenty-five products made from timber. How many more products can you think of to add to it?

- baseball bats
- beams
- blocks
- boats
- bowls
- clapboards
- clothespins
- fences
- furniture
- handles
- hockey sticks
- mixing spoons
- musical instruments
- oars
- paper towels
- pencils
- pennant sticks
- pianos
- shingles
- signposts
- spools
- toilet paper
- toothpicks
- toys
- writing paper

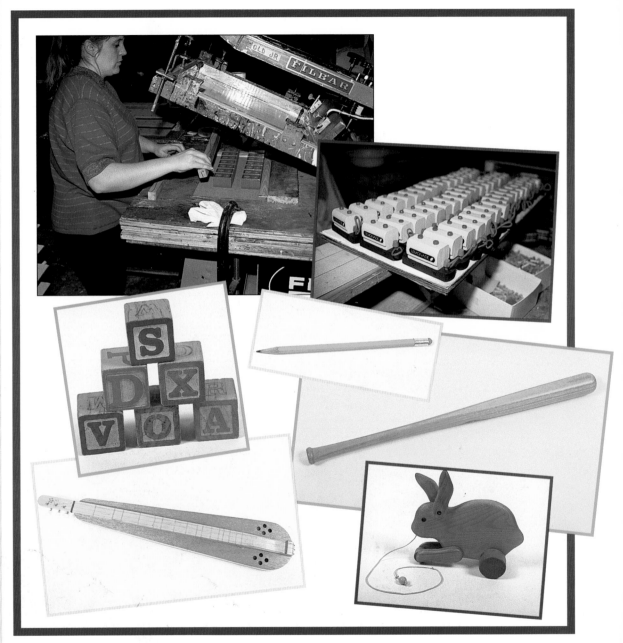